# ENJOY
# LIFE

Copyright © Richard Pearce, 2012

Published 2012 by CWR, Waverley Abbey House, Waverley Lane, Farnham, Surrey GU9 8EP, UK.
Registered Charity No. 294387. Registered Limited Company No. 1990308.

The right of Richard Pearce to be identified as the author of this work has been asserted by him in
accordance with the Copyright, Designs and Patents Act 1988.

All rights reserved. No part of this publication may be reproduced, stored in a retrieval system,
or transmitted, in any form or by any means, electronic, mechanical, photocopying, recording or
otherwise, without the prior permission in writing of CWR.

For a list of our National Distributors, visit www.cwr.org.uk

Unless otherwise indicated, all Scripture references are from the Holy Bible: New International
Version (NIV), copyright © 1973, 1978, 1984 by the International Bible Society.

Other version used:
AV: Authorised Version

Editing, design and production by CWR

Printed in Croatia by Zrinski

ISBN: 978-1-85345-666-4

Full of quotes and sayings to help you

# { ENJOY LIFE }

RICHARD PEARCE

**CWR**

In memory of
Marjorie Fargher Pearce
1919–1996

# CONTENTS

# LIFE'S HARD!

*Success isn't automatic*
This book of *practical*, easy to follow
tips is designed to help you

## ENGOY

### Life

**Get more out of LIFE**

more fun
more enjoyment
more satisfaction

**FOR ANYONE**
who wants to …

more time
more efficiency
more success

• get organised
• enjoy more success

**with God's help.**

more meaning
more purpose
more hope

'I can do everything
through him who
gives me strength'
Philippians 4:13

# A TRUE STORY

No one expects their plane to fall thousands of feet through the air and crash into a freezing river without loss of life, but this is what happened in New York in 2009.

Six minutes into the flight, the aircraft lost all power after hitting a flock of Canadian geese. The pilot and crew were hailed as heroes for helping all 150 passengers escape the stricken plane before it was submerged in the icy Hudson River in just *thirty minutes*.

There are many television documentaries which feature air crash survivor interviews, but the one I saw after this particular event really made me think. A passenger of the failed US Airways flight 1549 told how this experience had changed his life. What was his new outlook on life? It was simply this: 'ENJOY LIFE … live for today, *don't wait for tomorrow.*'

# WRITTEN FOR YOU

This is not a detailed discussion or a textbook but an *easy to read* collection of quotes, wise sayings and practical tips.

Written to REMIND US of great ideas that we may have heard, but DON'T put into practice …

**Yet.**

The *challenge* is to stop and ask ourselves:

- Do I already do this?
- Is it working for me?
- Am I really enjoying life?

'do not merely listen to the word … Do what it says'

James 1:22

'since my youth, O God, you have taught me, and to this day I declare your marvellous deeds.'

Psalm 71:17

# THE AUTHOR

Born in Birmingham, England's second largest city, I have two older brothers, and grew up with very few 'luxuries'. I scraped through grammar school to start a tough four-year apprenticeship in the building trade. I accumulated a total of twenty-one years working 'on the tools', including running my own small, but successful, home improvement business. I met and married the lovely Wendy in the 1980s. Our daughter Jenni now works with me for a local home additions builder. (This book was originally written for Jenni's 21st birthday.)

We moved to Canberra in 1999 and are all blessed to be here. Now fully-fledged Aussies, we even drink *cold* beer! Life has had its fair share of challenges (my father left the family when I was four), but emigrating has given us all a new lease of life. I've even won a few sales awards along the way. Australia has been good to us.

Family, friends and *especially* faith play a big part in our lives. A day of rest, once a week, has to be good!

My wonderful mother, Marjorie, seemed to have an endless supply of wise sayings, many of which are included here. The idea to write a book of these life lessons first occurred to me as a young boy.
Now, after many years … here it is!

**'Enjoy'**

## HOW THIS BOOK CAN HELP **YOU**

This is a WORKBOOK not just to read, but for you to mark the best parts. Designed to help you 'come up higher' and really …

**ENJOY** LIFE

'turning life's lessons into life skills'

- Highlight or <u>underline</u> any points that really stand out for you

- Fold the top corner to recap later

- Make notes if necessary

But most important

- **TRY OUT** some ideas … today

# ENJOYING LIFE
# EVERY DAY

ENJOY LIFE, it's the only one you have!
*'One life to live, no time to lose!'*
No one else can live your life for you.
**IT'S UP TO YOU** …

It really pays to stop and think about what
we're doing with our time here on earth.

Life can be hard (I have back pain now),
however … *we are allowed to enjoy life.*

*We just need a little help from
time to time.*

'it's never
too late'

# GETTING STARTED ...
## ENJOY TODAY

**ENJOY LIFE**

'ONE DAY AT A TIME.'
That's all it takes to get started ...

'therefore do not worry about tomorrow, for tomorrow will worry about itself. Each day has enough trouble of its own'
Matthew 6:34

# THE CHALLENGE TO SUCCEED

*Why don't we listen* to great advice?
Do we think we know it already?
Or are we lazy?
'We've heard it all before …
but we don't practise it at all!'
Familiarity breeds contempt.

As you read, stop and ask yourself …
Is this a good idea? Can I use it?
A challenge to succeed will then lead
to a choice …

'are you ready for more success?'

# LIFE

# Why not enjoy it?

'however many
years a man may live,
let him enjoy them all'
Ecclesiastes 11:8

Before you start, please don't forget ... fold down the top corner of any page you enjoy, as you go.

- Reading will only get you so far

  ✗——————→ to here.

- Reviewing will get you further

  ✗————————————————————→ to here.

- Making notes will help even more ...

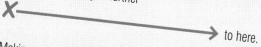

ENJOY LIFE

'great results are GUARANTEED!'

# You're talented

*gifted*

Everyone has their own special talent or gift, but not everyone *discovers* it.
If you **FEEL STRONGLY** about something that you can **DO EASILY**, then you may have *found your talent!*

Know your strengths and build on them. This will bring you much more success … *Skill* is what you learn. *Talent* is from above.

'don't hide your talent'

# Has anyone told you ...

'you are no accident. God knew what He was doing when He made you'

## 'You're amazing'

# yet?

(Well, consider yourself told!)

# You have potential
## *all your own*

Everyone does!
But **YOURS** is **SPECIAL**.
It's unique to you!
'No one can do what you can
do, the way you do it!'

Ask yourself …
Am I just sitting on my potential
– or learning daily?
How could I improve even more?
Write down your answer …

'use it or lose it'

# Something new

*could change your life!*

When was the LAST time you did something for the FIRST TIME? The fact is we get stuck in our old ways. We're comfortable with our 'safe' methods. Thinking like this can hold us back!

*This book is designed to challenge you …* Some of the ideas may be new. *Some you may have heard before*, but be willing to *try out* a few … today.

'take a leap of faith'

# Confidence
## *and how to get it*

Confidence comes from *trying* something you're inexperienced at *and succeeding*. Don't be afraid of trying something new or pushing through obstacles. Keep trying.

**FACE YOUR FEARS** ...
and do it anyway!
Think of something you need to do, but would rather put off. *Do it now*.
Success leads to confidence.

'... the LORD will be your confidence ...'
Proverbs 3:26

# Enthusiasm

*God in you*

**PASSION.** *The vital ingredient.* It's how you get promoted, give great service, sell more, break records and win awards. You need passion in your life.

Do what you're good at. Work for people who appreciate you. Celebrate your successes. Enjoy life! **GET ENTHUSIASTIC.**

'whatever your hand finds to do, do it with all your might ...' Ecclesiastes 9:10

# Have fun
## at work

Want to make your work easier?
Do your best. Be conscientious.
But don't forget also to
**HAVE FUN**.
If you do, you're more likely to
enjoy work and less likely to quit.

Remember, work hard
AND have fun.
Try to include both in every day.
Or find another job …
And don't take yourself too
seriously.

'… the joy of the LORD is your strength'
Nehemiah 8:10

# Be creative
*live life in colour*

It's OK to be creative. Whether you're a natural or not, why not give it a go?
The world needs more creativity. At home, at work and at play.

Look for creative ways to express your thoughts and ideas.
Don't leave it all to the pros.
*Enjoy a little creativity today.*

'[God] is able to do immeasurably more than all we ask or imagine ...' Ephesians 3:20

# Less is more

# Simplify
## your life

Take a complicated world. Add even more detail and you have *a recipe for disaster!* How can we possibly achieve excellence if we're bogged down in unnecessary detail?

SIMPLIFY or de-clutter your life. Do the basics really well and excel! Using this method helped me achieve a lot and will help you too. Guaranteed.

'keep it simple …'

# Don't flap
## *or panic*

Have you ever seen an eagle fly?
They don't flap and run around
like a bush turkey!
They **WAIT** …
then rise on the thermals.
They're often seen soaring
on the heights.

**How can I apply
the same principle?**

'… those who hope in
the LORD will renew their
strength. They will soar on
wings like eagles; they will
run and not grow weary,
they will walk and not be
faint' Isaiah 40:31

# Stop and think
*before acting*

Henry Ford said, 'Thinking is hard, that's why most people don't do it.' Others overanalyse (sometimes called 'binge thinking'!). A little thought goes a long way …

Think carefully BEFORE you decide.
Is there a better way, which could save time, effort or even money?
Look for the best solution.
**THINK FIRST**.

> '"everything is permissible for me" – but not everything is beneficial' 1 Corinthians 6:12

# Save time
## think twice

Tired of *always rushing*?
No time to stop?
We all have the same
24 hours in a day.
How you use them is *up to you*.

Don't take on *too much*.
(You can't do everything.)
Avoid unnecessary travelling.
(Don't just jump in the car
and go.)
Think twice ... then act!

'spend your time wisely –
you can't get it back'

# Too busy?
## love to, but ...

Tired of demanding people?
Everyone wanting your time?
Never-ending work?
Well if *time is our most valuable resource*, why do we give it away so freely?

Sometimes we say 'yes' just to look good. 'No' is acceptable to reasonable people. The others will just have to wait ... we want to keep our sanity!
**SAY NO!**

'fear of man will prove to be a snare' Proverbs 29:25

Don't be a 'people pleaser' – see Psalm 56

# Timing is everything

It just is!

# Effective or efficient
## spot the difference

Efficiency is doing the job right.

**EFFECTIVENESS** is doing the **RIGHT JOB**.

Know the difference between the two and it will **BOOST** your performance.
It's simple!
Are you **effective**?

'make sure the ladder you're climbing
is not leaning on the wrong wall!'

# Have a plan
## get organised

'Plan the work and
work the plan.'
This simple step enables you to
**ACHIEVE MORE**
and feel less stressed.
Remember the five Ps – **P**roper
**P**reparation **P**revents **P**athetic
**P**erformance!

Start with a plan.
Shortlist the things you need
to do in order of importance,
the day before.
Allow time for unexpected
events but follow the plan
for better results.

'commit to the LORD whatever you do, and
your plans will succeed' Proverbs 16:3

# S P A C E

*room to move*

Leave a breathing s p a c e between jobs.

There's no need to *cram* each day.

Unexpected things *will* come up …

andfillthegaps.

'go with the flow'

# Prioritise
## first things first

Don't forget to prioritise jobs. Avoid the 'tyranny of the urgent'.

Don't ignore the important things. Especially when there's too much to do and not enough time … Do you ever have days like that? This will help.

'keep the main thing the main thing'

# Start your day
*right*

All too often we get up late and have to rush out of the house. Or is it just me? **A MORNING ROUTINE** really helps ... especially if sometimes you wake up *slow*!

'start as you mean to go on'

Here are a few suggestions ...
- Get up! Put your feet on the floor
- Enjoy a good breakfast. Drink water
- READ/PRAY or both
- Stretch/exercise
- Plan to stop for lunch

Don't stay up too late. Get things ready for the next day. Try to go to bed the same day that you got up!

# Don't be distracted
## have a 'laser-like' focus

Too many times in life we take our eye off the ball and miss out. In order to accomplish great things we need to *resist distractions*.

Eg: Unnecessary dramas, unnecessary phone calls or emails. Literally days can be wasted on things that are urgent – but *not important*.

'multitasking is overrated'

# Can't decide?
## don't freeze

Are you someone who analyses *everything*? Are you always thinking, but unable to decide what to order for lunch? If symptoms persist, quit analysing!

*The paralysis of analysis* is a real problem. It will slow you down when you need to be decisive – and annoy your friends! Just decide (try the focaccia) … and **LIGHTEN UP**!

'don't sweat the small stuff'

# Just do it
## don't procrastinate

Have you heard this one – 'don't put off till tomorrow what you can do the next day'? I was going to procrastinate … but I thought I'd leave it till later!

If something needs to be done, why not do it straightaway? Otherwise nothing gets done and you'll just have a long to-do list! **DO IT NOW**. Have less to do later.

'D.I.N. – do it now!'

# Don't rush
## a task

'More haste, less speed.'
I don't know about you, but
I find that if I rush,
it only leads to mistakes.
It's like a super-fast typist who
has to backspace and rewrite
all the time. Looks impressive,
but …

Slow down.
**WORK HARD NOT FAST**.
Think about what you're doing.
Concentrate and get it
*right first time*.

'all hard work brings a profit, but mere talk
leads only to poverty' Proverbs 14:23

# Finish
## what you started

This was drilled into me as an apprentice:
**Finish the job that you started**.
You can't achieve an excellent result unless you actually *finish*.
It's impossible.
I'm off out now!
I'll finish this later ...!

Business advisors and mental health experts say,
'**DON'T START** a new job until you've finished what you're doing.'
Anyway, no one wants to finish your work.
See it through to the end.

'done!'

# 100% Perfect

*never*

Not possible.
Doesn't exist.
Do yourself a favour and …
**GIVE UP ON PERFECTIONISM**.
Do a great job but don't waste
your time *striving* for perfection.
*It's a killer!*

Freedom and success don't
come from doing something
100% perfectly.
*Sometimes* you just have to
let go and say,
'That's my best, for now.'

'near enough is near enough'

# Tidy up
## your mess

Why live in a disorganised mess where you can't always find what you need?
I know some people are naturally messy, but there is a limit. Or … if you had to move house quickly, could you do it?

'A place for everything, and everything in its place.'
'Clean as you go.'
It's easy and it pays off when you feel better afterwards. Take time to tidy up. *Now?*

'cleanliness is next to godliness'

# Set yourself a goal

*Any **worthwhile** goal.*
Write it down.

Set a time limit.
Make it realistic.

'go for it!'

# Chart your progress
## you can't lose

- ✓ Take clothes to charity shop
- ✓ Write Christmas cards
- Complete application form
- Book a holiday

'and display in a
prominent position'

# Celebrate!

*your successes*

Celebrate your successes!
Always.
What's the point, otherwise?
Even a small celebration
will work …
*Enjoy the moment.*

I'm going to celebrate.
I've just finished my first book!
Well, maybe in the morning …
(it's a bit late now).

'LORD, you establish peace for us; all that we have accomplished you have done for us' Isaiah 26:12

# Problems, problems
## *problems*

Life has its ups and downs. Sometimes all at once! We ALL have problems and challenges, but as someone said, 'that's when you learn …'

It's how we *respond* that counts. Don't deny or ignore your problems, *face them head on*. (With God's help, I suggest.) Start with baby steps and persevere …

'a righteous man may have many troubles, but the LORD delivers him from them all …' Psalm 34:19

# Feelings

*can you trust them?*

Sometimes when things are *tough* and everything seems *too much* … you've just gotta **HOLD ON**! Success can be just around the corner. 'The night is darkest just before sunrise.'

Don't wait till you feel better. Press on regardless. Just keep going (see no. 53).

'he gives strength to the weary and increases the power of the weak' Isaiah 40:29

# Catharsis
## *a listening ear*

'It's not what you eat;
it's what's eating you!'
Bottling up worries
will usually do you harm.
Talking them through
is *cathartic*.
You may not need advice,
just a chance to talk.

Don't carry the burden alone.
'A problem shared is
a problem halved.'
**TALK** to someone.
You'll probably feel
a lot better afterwards.
That's catharsis.

'cast your cares on the LORD and he will sustain you …' Psalm 55:22

'… there is a friend who sticks closer than a brother …' Proverbs 18:24

# Rest for the weary

'Come to me, all you who
are weary and burdened, and I will
give you rest. Take my yoke upon
you and learn from me, for I am
gentle and humble in heart, and you
will find rest for your souls. For my
yoke is easy and my burden is light.'

Matthew 11:28–30

# Ask for help
## and help others

Feel like you're going under?
Too much to do and
not enough time?
Stressed?

**HELP IS AT HAND.**

*Delegate.* Even if you think
you could do it better,
or quicker, yourself.
Ask for help.
Don't be embarrassed;
synergy works.
Help others.

'as iron sharpens iron, so one man
sharpens another' Proverbs 27:17

# Take advice

*listen*

No one likes a smart aleck.
Don't think you know it all.
You don't.
We still have A LOT to learn.
Even sporting champions
have a coach!

There are plenty of people
around who can help us.
If we look for them.
'Don't try to BE an expert –
GET an expert!' Listen to advice.
(Husbands, listen to your wives!)

'the way of a fool seems right to him, but a
wise man listens to advice' Proverbs 12:15

# Opportunity
## *or crisis*

'You're fired!' It's not what you want to hear, but it could be a great opportunity.
(It was for me, more than once.)
Did you know that in Chinese the same symbol is used for 'crisis' and 'opportunity'?

Life often throws up opportunities that are disguised as challenges.
'Opportunity is better seized than created.'
If a friend wants to meet up …
SAY YES!
And 'Strike while the iron's hot!'

> *'carpe diem –*
> *seize the day'*

# Why stress?
*breathe*

I remember when stress was a building term. Now it seems part of everyday life! If you find yourself stressed, it may be time to pause and 'come up for air'. Hopefully this book will help.

Pressure is good. It makes us perform. But too much pressure equals stress, which is toxic. We need to accept the one and reject the other.

'do not wear yourself out to get rich; have the wisdom to show restraint' Proverbs 23:4

# Need a break?

*press pause*

When the pressure is mounting
and you feel the fun is gone …
*don't just keep going.*
**Stop, revive, survive.**

- Look out of the window
- Get up and move around
- Talk to someone
- Switch your phone off!
- Watch or read a funny email
- Phone a friend
- Make a cuppa
- Pray
- Laugh

Then get back into it!

'come up
for air'

# Time for yourself
## today is all we have

'There is a part of **EVERY DAY** that is rightfully yours to enjoy.' A few minutes doing something for yourself will work wonders.

Why not take 'time-out' or 'me time'. For example – walk in the park, see an exhibition or just enjoy a coffee break. It's OK to do something for you.

'… I have come that they may have life, and have it to the full' John 10:10

# Day of rest

*once a week*

Fancy taking *a whole day to rest* once a week? No work allowed. How refreshing! Impossible? Well, it's what we were designed for.

Can't afford to? Can't afford not to! A lot of people know this secret. Sadly, a lot of Christians don't. STOP WORKING and rest. Then you won't burn out!

'... on the seventh day [God] rested ...' Genesis 2:2

# The simple things
## wake up and smell the roses

Remember, the **BEST** things
in life are **FREE**.
'Never be so busy making a living
that you forget to make a life.'
This saying hangs above my desk
to remind me, *don't miss out.*

Why not … go for a bike ride,
walk in the fresh air, go to the
lake, lie beneath a tree or just
*stop and take in the view*?

'what is this life if, full of care, we have no time to stand and
stare' From 'Leisure', a poem by W.H. Davies (1871–1940)

# Tempus fugit
## time flies

Ever notice how time flies?
You think of doing something,
then it's too late.
Why wait until you retire
to enjoy life? Or, as an old
workmate of mine used to
say, 'Why wait till you're
incontinent?!'

Enjoy the life you have
here and now.
**BEFORE IT'S TOO LATE**.
Book a holiday or go out with
your family!
Think you don't have time?
Buy a ticket!

'the sooner you go, the longer the
memories' Tourism Australia TV ad

# Plan a day trip
*a quick getaway*

Tired of the old routine? Need a break? Consider a day out. Get away from where you live or work, and get refreshed.

It doesn't have to be far, the next town or beach will do. It doesn't have to be long, half a day will do. Just book a day in the diary and stick to it!

'variety is the spice of life'

# Solitude

*downtime*

In this world of busyness, have we forgotten solitude? We all need TIME ALONE to collect our thoughts, focus or renew our energy.

Solitude need not be lonely. It can be one of the kindest things we can do for ourselves and those around us. Sit on a hill or in a café – both are good.

'… Jesus often withdrew …'

Luke 5:16

# Smell the roses
## listen to the birds

Look at the *stars* at night –
there are millions!

Watch the *sunset* at dusk –
it only lasts for 20 minutes.

Marvel at the *countryside* –
and the stunning views.

'Stop and smell the roses.'
**ENJOY** the amazing beauty
of creation.

'the earth is the LORD's, and
everything in it ...' Psalm 24:1

# Hope
*for the future*

'It's not the bad things that get us down, but the **LACK OF GOOD THINGS**.' We all need something to look forward to, like a long weekend or a party.

Buy a concert ticket. Plan a picnic. Meet friends at the weekend. I'm looking forward to heaven … What are you looking forward to?

'hope deferred makes the heart sick …'

Proverbs 13:12

# Improve your mood
## refuse to give up

get up! have breakfast

read something inspiring

pray and worship

s t r e t c h

rest or lie down

get dressed!

talk to someone

(wife/kids/flat mate)

plan your day

tidy up, clear your desk

go and sit or walk outside

play with the dog

phone a friend or loved one

book a night out – Friday?

review your successes

do something you love

put the kettle on!

play some music … loud!

write, draw or create …

'refuse to give up or feel sorry for yourself'

If you think you are beaten. → **you are**

If you think you dare not. → **you don't**

If you like to win, but you think you can't,

It's almost certain → **you won't ...**

For out of the world we find,

Success begins with a fellow's will.

**It's all in the state of mind**

Walter D. Wintle,
from the poem 'Thinking'
(early twentieth century)

# Stay positive
## making the right choices

Life is hard.
We're surrounded by bad news.
*Staying positive must be
a priority* if we're going to
overcome and win.
Look for the optimist's viewpoint
… *even if you're a natural
pessimist.*

Here's how.
Eat, sleep and exercise well.
Take time for yourself.
Listen to music/read.
*Avoid very negative people.*
Make friends.
Go out more …

'… whatever is noble … think
about such things' Philippians 4:8

# Stuck in the seventies
## *or the 80s*

Have you heard this one?
'The older I get, the better I was!'
Don't be STUCK IN THE PAST.
Things are very different now.
Do you need to catch up?

Memories of good times can be
great but don't live in the past.
Let it go. Move on.
Stay relevant or get left behind!

'welcome to the twenty-first century!'

# Keep learning
*improve your life*

*Some people never learn!*
They're still doing what they did
when they were younger.
And things are not improving …

The best way to grow is
to *keep learning*.
Look for opportunities
to learn *every day*.
READ MORE, or better
still, STUDY.
Attend courses or
inspiring talks.
Refusing to learn is fatal!
Be teachable.

{ 'you never get to complete
your education' }

# No more excuses
## take responsibility

Mental health starts with us *taking responsibility for our own actions*. We can't spend life blaming others for our problems, or expecting someone else to come along and fix them for us.

'**LIFE IS WHAT YOU MAKE IT**'.
Carve out a better lifestyle for yourself.
Pursue your dream.
Use the tips in this book and take action!

'God helps those who help themselves'

# I'm only human
## *we all make mistakes*

Please …
don't be too hard on yourself.
We all make mistakes.
We're only human.
Don't let mistakes of the past
hold you back today.

Next time you remember
something, don't say 'I'm so
stupid, I *forgot* …'
Try saying 'Oh good, I
*remembered* …'
**BE KIND TO YOURSELF**.

'… forgetting what is behind …
I press on …' Philippians 3:13–14

# Bounce back
*quickly*

A real sign of **MATURITY** is being able to *recover quickly from a setback*. Feeling pain or loss is quite normal. *Dwelling* on a problem for *too long* is immature and harmful to your health.

'A setback does not mean defeat.'
Get over it. As soon as possible.
*Never hold a grudge* or stay bitter.
Forgive if you need to …
Move on.

'dust yourself off and
get back on your feet'

# Don't give up
## be determined

Three small words –
**JUST ... KEEP ... GOING**
Things will improve.

Even if you feel down (like I did today), *don't give up*. Remember, there's always someone worse off than you (or me). Rest. Do something you love to do. Keep smiling ☺ and PERSEVERE!

'blessed is the man who perseveres under trial ...' James 1:12

# Grow up!
## it's time

**ARE YOU MATURE? Let's see …**
Do you get impatient, defensive or moody?
How do you behave if you don't get your way?
Can you take criticism … or compliments?
Do you *forgive* or *apologise* quickly?

Challenging isn't it?
'Age is compulsory but maturity is optional.'
First we need to grow up. Then we will be able to teach others.

'when I was a child, I talked like a child, I thought like a child, I reasoned like a child. When I became a man, I put childish ways behind me' 1 Corinthians 13:11

# Be a leader
## step up

**A leader is someone who …**
Knows what to do next ◄
Knows why ◄
Knows which resources to use ◄

If people need you to lead …
**TAKE CHARGE**.
*Make decisions, quickly and decisively.*
Lead others. Build the team.
The leader is the one who shouts, 'Let's go!'

{ 'if you're NOT a natural leader, don't volunteer' }

# Pride v humility
## watch out!

No matter how successful you are, *you still need to be humble*. This is hard, I know, but a very necessary fact of life.

Avoid pride at all costs because …
'God opposes the proud but gives grace to the humble' (James 4:6).

'humble yourselves before the Lord, and he will lift you up' James 4:10

# First impressions
*count a lot!*

Can you finish this sentence:
'You never get a second
chance to ...'?
When meeting new people,
the first few seconds *really*
count, especially in business.
We can often judge people
instantaneously!

Stand up when you
greet people.
(A *firm* handshake helps.)
Keep eye contact. SMILE.
Repeat names to help
remember them.
Be awake! (And be prepared.)

{ 'you never get a second chance to
make a first impression' }

# Smile more
## and be friendly

Everyone loves a friendly face. It's much better than the alternative. A smile ☺ will open doors for you. A smile will cost you nothing. A smile ☺ is infectious!

Develop your sense of humour. Ask for God's help; I did! People respond better to a friendly person, and especially one who shows them respect.

'a cheerful look brings joy to the heart …'
Proverbs 15:30

# Be interesting
*and interested*

Don't be boring!
**Be interesting**.
Join in the conversation.
And smile.

**Be interested** in others
and what they have to say.
Ask questions.

This is basic communication.
It's simple … but simply
beautiful.

'each of you should look not only to your own interests,
but also to the interests of others' Philippians 2:4

# Listen first
## *then speak*

Often the best help is
to listen to others.
To *really listen* shows we care.
After all, everyone wants to
be understood.

Listen with your eyes.
Focus on the other person (not
on what you want to say next).
*Reflect back* what you think
you heard.
*Ask relevant questions* then
**LISTEN** to the answers.

'... everyone should be quick to listen,
slow to speak ...' James 1:19

# Short and sweet
*be succinct*

**Get to the point!**
Don't be boring!
No one likes too many words.
Especially men!
*People lose interest.*
Enjoy better conversations
by not talking *too much*.
(Try listening?)

Conversation should be a *two-way process*.
Don't dominate or 'hijack'
a conversation.
LEARN TO SUMMARISE.
Always check the response
of the listener …

'the more the words, the less the
meaning …' Ecclesiastes 6:11

# P's and Q's
## pls & thx

'Please', 'thank you' and 'excuse me'. It's what we were taught as a child. We may not be holding doors open as much, but *manners still count.* A lot.

*People will respect you more* if you're NOT RUDE. (You usually get better service when you're kind to the staff.)
Why not give someone a thank you gift?
Or just send them a text ☺

'... do to others what you would have them do to you ...' Matthew 7:12

# Don't be selfish
## it makes you ugly

Selfishness is **UGLY**. And it's a sure way to lose friends and alienate people! Selfishness is the world's WORST attitude. People can see it in us, long before we do. Get your mind off yourself, *and feel better.*

Start by listening more and talking less. *Put other people's interests first* and you'll become more attractive! (See no.59.)

{ '... love your neighbour as yourself'
Matthew 22:39 }

# Be generous
## and help others

I have my wife to thank for teaching me this. She's amazing! You can help others and still have enough. 'You make a living by what you get … you make a LIFE by what you GIVE.'

Don't just give your old broken things or leftovers. That's not generosity! Give of your time, money, food, clothes, car etc. Try it. Look for ways to help others. Be creative.

'… it is more blessed to give than to receive' Acts 20:35

# Choose friends
*carefully*

Choose your friends carefully. We are all *under the influence* of somebody. Be around people you look up to. People who **INSPIRE YOU**.

The Bible says that 'friendship with the world is hatred towards God' (James 4:4) Spend time with some people who you **WANT TO BE LIKE** (who lift you up).

'... bad company corrupts good character'
1 Corinthians 15:33

'he who walks with the wise grows wise ...'
Proverbs 13:20

# Phone a friend
## *keep in touch*

One of the *most underrated pleasures* in life is having friends. *Friends are vital* for many reasons. Don't live without friends. Cultivate great friendships.

'You've got to **BE** a friend to **HAVE** a friend.' **STOP** reading this now. Phone, text or email someone you know. Make the effort and … **DO IT NOW**.

'make time for friends'

WELL ...
**DID YOU DO IT?**
Did you call, email
or text someone?

*yes!*

WELL DONE!

*no*

I just messaged a friend and it works!
We're meeting for lunch on Sunday.

**If not**,
don't go to the
next page ...
**DO IT NOW.**

'you've got to
BE a friend to
have a friend'

# Be reliable
## *dependable*

Please …
If you say you're gonna do it …
*Then do it.*
If you say you'll be there …
*Be on time.*

People are looking for someone they can depend on.
You can **BE THAT PERSON**.
Follow through, do a good job.
It's worth the effort.

'am I unreliable?'

# Your attitude
*it's your choice*

Did you know your attitude can make or break you? 'Attitude determines ALTITUDE.' If you want to be the best that you can be, first choose a really good attitude.

Work on having a grateful, 'can do' attitude.
Always keep a **positive mental attitude**. (See no.47.)
Give yourself regular checkups.

'... be made new in the attitude of your minds ...' Ephesians 4:23

## Attitude checkup

'where would you like to improve?'

**Put an ✖ on the line where you think you sit now**

here ✖                    ✖ or here

overcomer ·········· ✖ ············ ✖ ······· victim

optimist ················································· pessimist

grateful ················································· whinger

focused ················································· vague

hardworking ············································· lazy

generous ················································ stingy

caring ··················································· selfish

teachable ·············································· know it all

forgiving ·············································· resentful

flexible ················································ stubborn

loving ·················································· critical

brave ··················································· chicken

co-operative ············································ maverick

team player

tidy ··················································· disorganised

# Integrity
*with God's help we can do it*

Always truthful
Open and honest
Reliable and dependable
Committed, loyal

High standards
Upright, humble
Honourable

'the integrity of the upright
guides them ...' Proverbs 11:3

# Appreciate
## what you have

Be grateful and 'count your blessings'.

**LIST THE TOP 10** things you enjoy.

(Here are mine to get you started.)

- Time with God. Being inspired.
- Learning and growing.
- Quality time with Wendy and Jen. Our home.
- Driving around Canberra.
- Building people up. Encouraging others.
- Being creative. Playing music and writing.
- Good health. Fun. Humour.
- Reading and coffee in a favourite café.
- Seeing friends at the weekend.
- Visiting new places.

'start your list now and see where it takes you'

# Satisfaction
*guaranteed?*

Some people are never satisfied. They say 'when XYZ happens **THEN I'LL BE HAPPY**.' Watch out, this is dangerous thinking! Remember, a lot of things *don't* satisfy.

Finish this sentence now: 'I'll be happy when

............................................'

(and check your response).

{ '... godliness with contentment is great gain' 1 Timothy 6:6 }

# CON TENT MENT

want to get rich?

'But godliness with contentment is great gain. For we brought nothing into the world, and we can take nothing out of it. But if we have food and clothing, we will be content with that. People who want to get rich fall into temptation and a trap and into many foolish and harmful desires that plunge men into ruin and destruction. For the love of money is a root of all kinds of evil. Some people, eager for money, have wandered from the faith and pierced themselves with many griefs.'

1 Timothy 6:6–10

# Success

*now*

What does it mean to be
'successful'?
There are many different views.
A newer car, bigger house,
top job etc.

Here's something new
to think about …
Instead of being successful
to be happy (some time
in the future) …
If you're **HAPPY**
you *are* **SUCCESSFUL**!

'… a man's life does not consist in the
abundance of his possessions' Luke 12:15

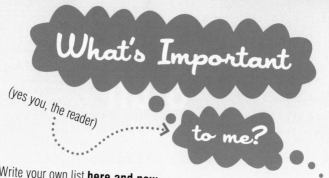

**What's Important**

*(yes you, the reader)*

**to me?**

Write your own list **here and now** ...

1.
...................................................................................................................................

2.
...................................................................................................................................

3.
...................................................................................................................................

4.
...................................................................................................................................

Write down any action required alongside each one.
**Follow through.**

# Stuff
## a challenge

What would you grab
in a house fire?
Could you decide in
just three minutes?
Photos? Documents? Valuables?
What do you have that you
cannot replace or do without?
Tough choice.

In the Canberra bushfires
in 2003, hundreds of people
lost everything, including
their homes.
After sifting through the ashes,
some said, 'It doesn't matter –
it's just stuff.'
(As I write this, a house in the
next street is ablaze!)

'it's just stuff'

'**PEOPLE ARE**
spending money they DON'T HAVE
on things they DON'T NEED
to impress people they DON'T LIKE.'

'credit is a new
name for debt'

# Money

*money, money*

'Whoever loves money never has money enough; whoever loves wealth is never satisfied …' (Ecclesiastes 5:10). Did you know that Jesus spoke more about money than He did about heaven?

Generally, we need to **SAVE** some, **SPEND** some and **GIVE** some away.
We're *stewards*, not owners. And anyway, you can't take it with you …

'keep your lives free from the love of money and be content …' Hebrews 13:5

# Rich and famous
## *it sucks!*

Famous people have it all … or do they? Did you know that the highest rate of suicide is among the rich and famous? It seems that money isn't everything.

The more you *have*, the more you *have to do*. Think about it. If money doesn't make you happy … *what does*?

'what good is it for a man to gain the whole world, yet forfeit his soul?' Mark 8:36

# More to life
*than this?*

**THERE HAS TO BE!**
Don't wait until your deathbed
to meet your Maker.
Don't leave it till it's too late!

Jesus said, 'I am the way
and the truth and the life'
(John 14:6). Do we really think
we can do it all successfully
without Him?
The fact is, everyone prays
in a crisis.
Why wait and miss out?

'… I have come that they may have life,
and have it to the full' John 10:10

# Who am I?
## the big question

'**WHO YOU ARE** is more important than what you **DO**' – ie we're human beings, not human doings. We're not defined by our *roles* but by our *character* and *personality*.

Each one of us is special and has different gifts, talents and abilities. You are more than the job you do. You are unique.
Be the very best that *you* can be.

'… I am fearfully and wonderfully made …'
Psalm 139:14

# Beliefs
## *true or false?*

'If you don't
**STAND** for something,
you'll **FALL** for anything.'
Beliefs are what shape us.
We think-believe-decide-
do-become.

**BE VERY CAREFUL**
what you believe.
Despite our advancing
technology, much of this
world still remains a mystery.
*Not everything we see
or hear is true.*
Some things we can
never really *know*.

'a simple man believes anything, but a prudent
man gives thought to his steps' Proverbs 14:15

For you created my inmost being;
  you knit me together in my
    mother's womb.
I praise you because I am fearfully
  and wonderfully made;
  your works are wonderful,
  I know that full well.
My frame was not hidden from you
  when I was made in the secret place.
When I was woven together in the
    depths of the earth,
  your eyes saw my unformed body.
All the days ordained for me
  were written in your book
  before one of them came to be.

Psalm 139:13–16

# Spirituality
*explained*

We are all *spirit*, soul and body (see 1 Thessalonians 5:23). But what does it mean to be *spiritual*? Is it being religious? No.

Want purpose and meaning? It's easy. It's all about …

- **BELONGING** to somebody
- Being **WORTH** something
- **SIGNIFICANCE** (being useful)

See the next page …

'… what is seen is temporary, but what is unseen is eternal' 2 Corinthians 4:18

# PURPOSE AND MEANING
## *Thanks*

to God the Father – **to whom *I belong***

to Jesus Christ – **whose life shows *my worth***

to the Holy Spirit – **who makes me *significant***

And all this is **FREE!** *The perfect gift.*

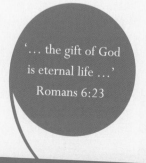

'… the gift of God
is eternal life …'
Romans 6:23

# No more faking
*be real*

Stop pretending that everything's OK, when *clearly* it's not.
**BE REAL!**
You don't have to impress … Most people *prefer honesty*.

If you're struggling, then say so. It's not 'all good' when you've just lost your job! That's just denial.

**Be yourself.**

'be authentic'

# Where do I turn?
## who do I turn to?

In times of trouble, who or what do I turn to? Food? TV? My computer? Or do I just withdraw? *Where we run to says a lot about us …*

'The name of the LORD is a strong tower; the righteous run to it and are safe.' Proverbs 18:10

'God is our refuge and strength, an ever-present help in trouble' Psalm 46:1

# Getting inspired
*it's easy!*

You don't have to
struggle on alone.
You can get inspired.
Inspiration is available to all.
(I was inspired to
write this book.)
Inspiration first,
then excellence.

You may have to wait.
You may have to ASK, but
inspiration has only one source.
**INSPIRATION COMES
FROM HEAVEN.**
The song 'Lean on me' just
played on the radio! *Cool*.

'you do not have, because you do
not ask God' James 4:2

# About prayer
## and meditation

It's like the air we breathe.
Essential.
'Seven days without prayer
makes one weak!'
You can say what you think.
It's that simple.
It's our opportunity to connect …

Prayer is **OPEN TO ANYONE**.
*Anytime, anywhere.*
Out loud or quietly. Nothing
complicated.
*Try it now, if you like …*
Meditation is simply
chewing over an idea till
all the flavour is out.

'… and whoever comes to me I will never
drive away' John 6:37

'This, then, is how you should pray:
"Our Father in heaven,
 hallowed be your name,
 your kingdom come,
 your will be done
   on earth as it is in heaven.
 Give us today our daily bread.
 Forgive us our debts,
   as we also have forgiven our debtors.
 And lead us not into temptation,
 but deliver us from the evil one."'

Matthew 6:9–13

# Who cares?
## our great calling

Knowledge is not enough. Training won't impress. Qualifications don't count either. Even if you have all the answers, there is one more essential characteristic needed. We need to **CARE FOR PEOPLE**.

'People don't care how much you know, till they know how much you care.'
Would you rather talk to an expert or an expert who really cares about you?

'if I … have not love, I am only … a clanging cymbal' 1 Corinthians 13:1

# Extraordinary

*not average*

The difference between
ordinary and extraordinary,
is that little bit EXTRA.
Don't just do the bare minimum
or be 'last in, first out'.

**BE EXTRAORDINARY**.
Do more than is required.
Arrive early. Help tidy up
afterwards.
Give generously.
Help others succeed.

'go the extra mile ...'
see Matthew 5:41–42

# Larger than life
## *be memorable*

**Colourful** characters are often interesting and they are the people we remember …
It doesn't mean being loud or eccentric for the wrong reasons …

**'DARE TO BE DIFFERENT.'**
*Don't be afraid* to step out of the crowd.
Be a tall poppy if you want.
It's OK to live life to the full.

'live the life you were meant to live'

# Meaning of life

*purpose*

Where am I **FROM**?
**WHY** am I here?
Where am I **GOING**?
These are the *most important questions* that we all want to know the answers to …

For real answers we need to look further than just other people's ideas.
We need to look to a higher source, to God's Word, the Bible.
It's all there waiting to be discovered …

'the unfolding of your words gives light …'
Psalm 119:130

# Get connected
## take part

Don't let life pass you by. There's so much available other than work, eat and sleep. *Don't go it alone.* Get involved.

**GET OUT MORE**

Join a sports club … get fitter.

Try Toastmasters … communicate better.

Attend church … *practise your faith.*

'… God keeps him occupied with gladness of heart' Ecclesiastes 5:20

# Find a project
## hobby or interest

*Too tired* when you get home?
All work, no play?
You may need to find
**A PROJECT**.
It may take a while to
find something you're
passionate about, but it's
definitely worth a try.

For example, this book started
out as a few ideas, then became
a gift for my daughter.
It still continues to occupy my
spare time (and not so spare
time) as ideas develop. *Great fun!*

'sow your seed in the morning, and at evening let
not your hands be idle …' Ecclesiastes 11:6

# Knowledge/wisdom
## *a worthy aim*

'Experience doesn't produce wisdom, just an experienced person.' Knowledge isn't wisdom, neither is learning. Wisdom is knowing how to *use* knowledge.

We are all growing older ... but are we **GROWING WISER**? Do you want a goal that's worth pursuing? Make wisdom your goal.

'blessed is the man who finds wisdom ... she is more profitable than silver ...' Proverbs 3:13–14

# REVIEW ...
## and improve

'Smart people learn from their mistakes. Really smart people learn from the mistakes of others …'
Champions are the ones who take notes and then REVIEW THEM to reinforce the lessons learnt and improve performance.

Try this: **REVIEW**, **REFLECT** and **RESPOND**.
*Review* at the end of the year.
*Reflect*. Think about what worked (or didn't).
*Respond* with improved methods.
You can't lose!

'regular adjustments will help you *enjoy life*'

# LOOSE ENDS
## *thanks for reading*

- Study communication. Use words carefully
- Take a long lunch and watch the world go by
- Stretch yourself intellectually and physically
- Face your fears
- Say sorry quickly and easily (and mean it)
- Try fasting for a day (keep drinking)
- Have an open mind to great ideas
- *Know that God loves you*
- Persevere
- Count your blessings
- Share with others
- Do your best
- Have balance

'the only thing that counts is faith expressing itself through love.'
Galatians 5:6

**NOW GET ORGANISED ... and *really* enjoy life!**

# The End

*or a new beginning?*

# CLEVER SAYINGS
## NOT PREVIOUSLY INCLUDED

'Chance favours the prepared mind.'

'Keep your eye on the prize …'

'The way we see the problem is the problem.' Einstein

'Make the most of what you've got.'

'You don't miss it till it's gone.'

'Enjoy it while you can …'

'You train people how to treat you.'

'A lack of planning on your part does not constitute an emergency on my part.'

'Fifty per cent of success is turning up.'

'A little of what you fancy does you good.'

'If you don't ask, you don't get.'

'Progress has little do with speed and everything to do with direction.'

'Never let your wishbone go where your backbone should be.'

'Where there's a will, there's a way.'

'It's easy when you know how.'

'Quitters never win and winners never quit.'

'Two's company; three's a crowd.'

'Prevention is better than cure.'

## LAST WORD

'A man reaps
what he sows.'

Galatians 6:7

# FURTHER READING
## LOOK IT UP NOW?

Matthew 7:24–29 (The wise and foolish builders)
James 4 (Draw close to God)
The book of Proverbs also makes a great study.

*Every Day with Jesus* Bible-reading notes written by Selwyn Hughes, published by CWR.

The Bible is the bestselling book in the world!
Read **every day** and highlight the bits which speak to you – it works!

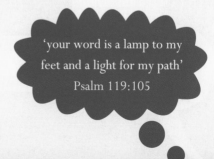

'your word is a lamp to my feet and a light for my path'
Psalm 119:105

# THE GREATEST
# SELF-HELP BOOK
## *in the world*

The
Holy Bible

'Get to know your
Bible. Or better
still, the Author!'

# BE BLESSED
## *enjoy Life*

'but the man who looks intently
into the perfect law that gives
freedom, and continues to do
this, not forgetting what he has
heard, but doing it – he will be
blessed in what he does.'

James 1:25

'taste and see that the LORD
is good; blessed is the man who
takes refuge in him'

Psalm 34:8

Courses and seminars

Publishing and new media

Conference facilities

# Transforming lives

CWR's vision is to enable people to experience personal transformation through applying God's Word to their lives and relationships.

Our Bible-based training and resources help people around the world to:
• Grow in their walk with God
• Understand and apply Scripture to their lives
• Resource themselves and their church

• Develop pastoral care and counselling skills
• Train for leadership
• Strengthen relationships, marriage and family life and much more.

Our insightful writers provide daily Bible-reading notes and other resources for all ages, and our experienced course designers and presenters have gained an international reputation for excellence and effectiveness.

CWR's Training and Conference Centre in Surrey, England, provides excellent facilities in an idyllic setting – ideal for both learning and spiritual refreshment.

**CWR** Applying God's Word *to everyday life and relationships*

CWR, Waverley Abbey House, Waverley Lane, Farnham, Surrey GU9 8EP, UK

Telephone: +44 (0)1252 784700
Email: info@cwr.org.uk
Website: www.cwr.org.uk

Registered Charity No 294387
Company Registration No 1990308